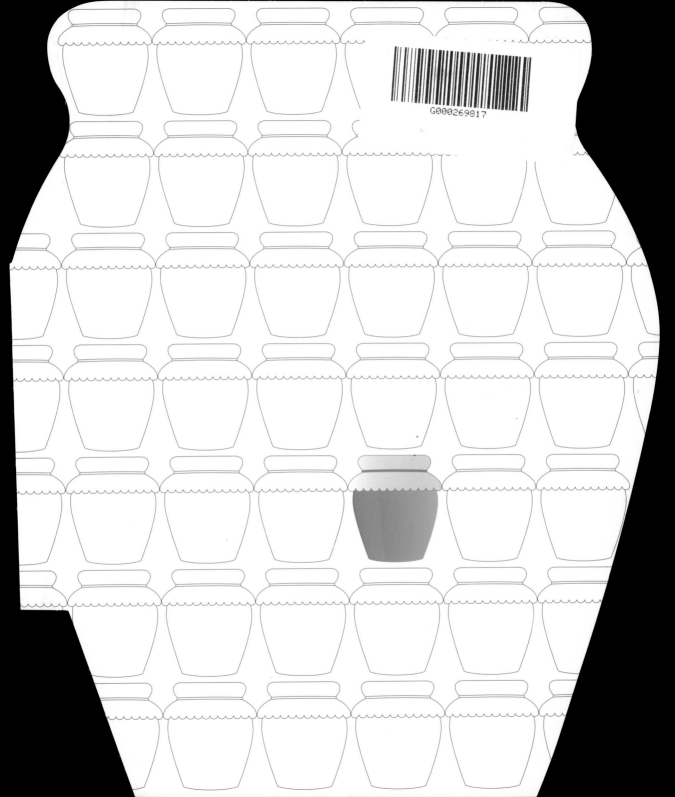

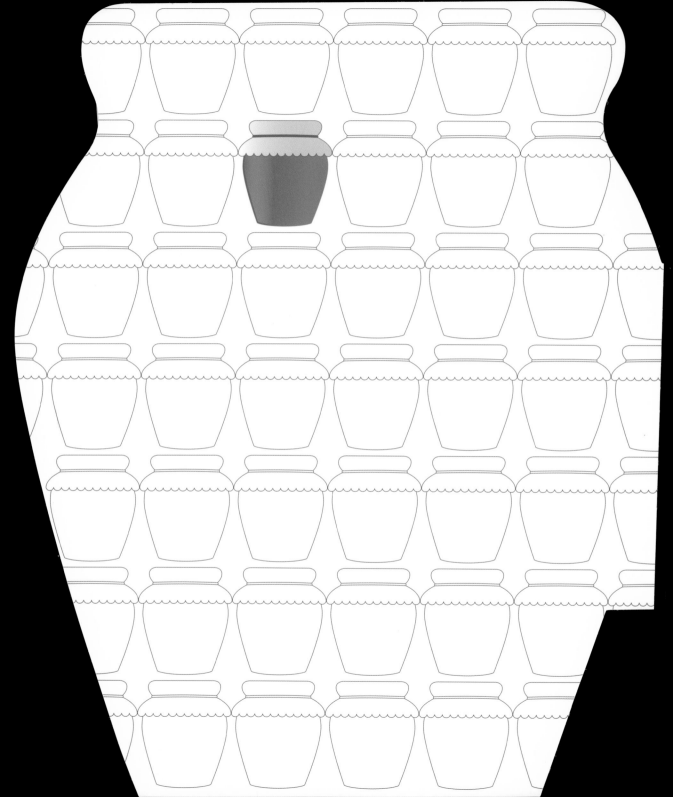

JAMS & PRESERVES

50 Easy Recipes

ACADEMIA
BARILLA

EDITED BY
ACADEMIA BARILLA

PHOTOGRAPHY BY
ALBERTO ROSSI
CHEF MARIO STROLLO
CHEF LUCA ZANGA

RECIPES BY
CHEF MARIO GRAZIA

TEXT BY
MARIAGRAZIA VILLA

GRAPHIC DESIGN
MARINELLA DEBERNARDI

EDITORIAL COORDINATION ACADEMIA BARILLA
CHATO MORANDI
ILARIA ROSSI
LEANNE KOSINSKI

CONTENTS

4

THE PLEASURE
OF MAKING IT AT HOME

I was sad, thinking about the future,
so I gave up and made myself some jam.
It's surprising how that lifts the spirits.

David Herbert Lawrence

Preserves are an invention for gluttonous, prudent souls. They hold the delicious wisdom of the heart: to keep the "here and now" for the less favorable seasons of the year, bringing out small precious gifts of flavor capable or bringing back the colors of the summer when there is snow outside, or the exuberance of spring as we enter the sweetness of autumn. Made at home, canning can immerse us in the joyful atmosphere of a ritual, perhaps worthy of the labor of Hercules but leaving a more emotional and gastronomic satisfaction, above all if we use vegetables or fruits from our own gardens. And if we do not work along, but enlist the help of the entire family, we share that priceless pleasure of transferring our creativity, affection and love to a glass jar. This is the space of a steaming, lively kitchen, filled with words, memories, jokes and pleasantries.

The ancient story of canning

From the time that the nomadic tribes settled down as farmers, man has felt the need to guarantee a food supply to enjoy at less fortunate times or places, or in times of famine or drought. To assure his survival, he came up with various forms of storing food, preventing it from perishing, honing culinary techniques and devising more and more evolved methods. At the beginning of this long adventure, where "need turned into virtue", he used the tools provided by nature: the wind, the sun and the heat, salt from the seas, smoke from the fire, snow and ice of winter. He later learned to cure foods so that they

could somehow last over time. From grapes he made wine, from olives he obtained olive oil, from milk cheese, from fresh meat came sausages, from wheat there was pasta. Drying, hot or cold smoking, salting, fermentation and refrigeration are just some of the methods invented by the ancient peoples to destroy or deactivate the microorganisms responsible for spoiling foodstuffs. However it is only now in the modern age that food preservation techniques have been perfected, no longer affecting the nutritional properties and organoleptic characteristics of fresh products as they increase food safety and prolong food life. The true revolution, which began to make canning foods reliable, was initiated by none other than Napoleon Bonaparte at the start of the 19th century. To be able to feed his armies, he promised an award of 12,000 francs to anybody who could invent a method to preserve foods for a long time, without dehydrating them. It was Parisian confectioner Nicolas Appert who won the prize with a technique that stored foods in sterilized glass jars, hermetically sealed and subjected to boiling water (a technique that had actually been invented a few years before by Italian naturalist Lazzaro Spallanzani).

The domestic art of preserving the "here and now"

Among the methods of home food preservation, sterilization by heat after bottling offers the greatest assurance: it not only aims to create an environment that is not friendly to microorganisms, but also destroys all those that are present as it renders substances responsible for fermentation and putrefaction, produced by the microorganisms, inactive. Heat sterilization consists of taking the food, contained in hermetically sealed vessels placed in a large pot fitted with a canning rack, at a temperature that is sufficiently high, on average between 210°F (100°C) and 250°F (120°C), for certain period of time. After the indicated time, the jars are left to cool in the sterilization water, and then again checked to assure that they are hermetically sealed.

Another excellent method is vacuum pack. In this technique, the food to be preserved, still hot, is placed in the glass jars which have been kept hot in the oven at a temperature of 210°F (100°C). The product is placed in the jars so a small space is left between the surface of the contents and the lid of the jar. This space should be around 1/2 inch (1 cm) for highly acidic foods such as fruit, and 4/5 inch (2 cm) for low acidic foods such as vegetables (this will compensate for the expansion of the cooked product and allow the formation of a vacuum as the jar cools). The containers are closed and turned over immediately in order to form the necessary vacuum, thereby increasing the shelf life of the food. The jars are left upside down to cool completely, and then they are ready for the pantry.

There are other methods that can easily be used at home to preserve foods. Preserving in oil uses the fatty properties of the food to isolate the food from contact with the air, and therefore from germs in the air. Pickling in alcohol on the other hand uses the ability of acetic acid or ethyl alcohol to create an environment that does not allow the development of microorganisms in food. Both salting, done by sprinkling salt over the product to be preserved, and pickling in brine or introducing the food into a saline solution, use the properties of the salt to penetrate the food tissues, causing a depletion of the water. Drying, the oldest form of preserving food adopted by man, uses the action of the sun to dehydrate the product to be preserved. In many cases this is combined with other preservation techniques: artichokes in oil for example are cooked in a solution of vinegar, wine and water, then left to dry in the sun, and finally placed in glass jars and covered with oil.

Sugar is also used either to impregnate or to cover the food, for example in the caramelization or candy-making technique, or added to fruit or vegetables in making jams. Sugar preserves the product perfectly, thanks to the presence of sucrose which prevents the growth of microorganisms responsible for deteriorating the food, absorbing excess moisture and forming an impassable barrier against microorganisms.

Tricks for a perfect canning

Once you have tasted homemade preserves you will never go back to store-bought preserves. And if it is true that a preserved food will never be like fresh, it is also true that at Christmas it is always better to enjoy a mango marmalade made with your own hands, rather than buying fresh mangoes from the other side of the world, frequently expensive and often tasteless.

For a good quality canned fruit or vegetables you must begin with the highest quality ingredients, gathered or purchased when they are "in season", when you can benefit from their maximum flavor and nutritional value, as well as at the best price. Mustard with white watermelon, for example, can be prepared in fall, as this is made from the fruit pulp and red seeds which is ripe beginning in September. Black-cherry jam on the other hand should be made in May or June, the two months when this fruit is in season and most flavorful. Oranges for marmalade are in season from November to April, or better yet in December or January, the best months for this citrus fruit.

More than selecting the perfect raw materials and perfect preparation of the recipe, knowing how to sterilize and correctly store the preserves is fundamental to prevent any infection or contamination that sometimes can be hazardous to your health. Regardless of the technique used to preserve your food, it is effective only if done correctly and with scrupulous attention.

One example is the lids. These must be in good condition, in particular if they have plastic or similar seals. Ideally you should also use new caps. The lid must be screwed on tight, but not too tight or the glass jars may break during the boiling water bath as the air is unable to escape. Once the lid has been closed, a sharp sound should result by tapping it with the handle of a spoon. A deaf sound and echo means that air has remained trapped in the jar, and this is not acceptable. If a jar has not sealed correctly, put it in the refrigerator and use the con-

tents within a few days. Once the preserves are completed, a sticker is affixed with the name of the preserve and the time (year) of preparation and the glass jars are placed in the pantry or in the basement, in a cool, dry place preferably not exposed to direct sunlight.

The contents are ready for consumption during a period that may range from a few months to a few years, depending on the type of preserves and the whether the conservation method was correctly followed. After the jar has been opened, the preserves must be used within 3 to 4 days.

Any change in the color or odor of the product, the presence of mold on the surface or a bulge or rust stain on the lid are clear indications that the food is not edible.

To sterilize empty jars and lids, see instructions on page 16. Empty jars used for vegetables, meats, and fruits to be processed in a pressure canner need not be presterilized. It is also unnecessary to presterilize jars for fruits, tomatoes, and pickled or fermented foods that will be processed 10 minutes or longer in a boiling-water canner.

Preserves in the kitchen

The joy of preparing genuine high quality preserves with your own hands is equaled only by being able to enjoy them either as a finished product or as an ingredient in the preparation of other foods or as an accompaniment for certain dishes.

There is nothing better than homemade preserves to give a personal and therefore unmistakable touch to any dish. It is that something extra that makes the difference. Raspberry jam, for example, is delicious just spread on a slice of bread; however it can also become the main ingredient of a tart. And if the raspberries were picked by you as you walked through the mountains, then washed, carefully dried and cooked with sugar to make a jam, your tart will have a taste that cannot be copied: one from your very heart.

In the kitchen, preserves are like a secret ingredient, a prism of opportunity that can be used successfully in any way that you want. Examples of this abound...

The characteristic Mostarda from Mantova, a kind of apple chutney made with a mustard flavored syrup, can be savored on its own.

However, by tradition, it is also served with roast beef or veal and is also excellent served with hard cheeses. It also forms part of the filling of pumpkin *tortelli*, a dish that dates back to Renaissance Mantua and now found in many areas of northern Italy. Bolete mushrooms in olive oil can give a special touch to an antipasto, can be used on a pizza or baked on focaccia, or used in a flavorful pasta. And giardiniera is perfect served alone to whet the appetite, but is even better served with grilled meat or a nice selection of cold cuts.

Peaches in syrup are excellent as the end to a good lunch or dinner, but they can also be combined with *panna cotta* (cooked cream), ice cream, chocolate, or amaretto, or they can become the fragrant filling of a pie or tart.

An Italian Tradition

Academia Barilla, an international center dedicated to disseminating Italian cuisine, has selected 50 recipes for this book of preserves, pastries and breads. In a culinary culture like ours, which is uniquely tied to the "tastes of home" and aims to maximize every product to help the home economy, preserves have been – and continue to be – one of the fundamental pillars.

Some of these recipes are well known and form part of the centuries old regional tradition of the Bel Paese: *cotognata* (quince jelly), for example, which is a specialty of Abruzzo, Puglia and Sicily, lemon marmalade and the compote of Tropea red onions, typical of Calabria, or the berry, black currant, raspberry and blueberry preserves of Trentino-Alto Adige.

Since the Middle Ages Italy has led in the preparation of jams, jellies, candied and caramelized fruits, thanks to the cultivation of sugar cane which was brought to Sicily by the Arabs in the 8th century, and the monopoly of the sugar trade held for centuries by Venice.

On the side of salty preserves is the glorious Italian tomato sauce. Born in Naples between the late 17th and early 18th century, this sauce was made from the pulp of red tomatoes, imported from the New World two centuries earlier.

It was first used in spaghetti, then pizza, and then was stored in glass jars or metal cans until later when other methods were found to preserve the sauce, guaranteeing the safe use of this red gold year round, either concentrated, peeled, chopped, in pasta or sauces.

The Perfect time to preserve

Following is a table of the fruits and vegetables and their best point for canning. Please remember these months may vary due to regional factors.

	JAN	FEB	MAR	APR	MAY	JUN	JUL	AUG	SEP	OCT	NOV	DEC
apples	•	•	•	•	•			•	•	•	•	•
apricots					•	•	•	•				
artichokes	•	•	•	•	•	•						
asparagus	•	•	•	•	•	•						
blueberries							•	•	•			
broccoli	•	•	•							•	•	•
cabbage	•	•	•	•	•	•	•	•	•	•	•	•
carrots	•	•	•	•	•	•	•	•	•	•	•	•
cauliflower	•	•	•	•						•	•	•

	JAN	FEB	MAR	APR	MAY	JUN	JUL	AUG	SEP	OCT	NOV	DEC
celery		•	•	•	•	•	•	•	•	•	•	
cherries					•	•						
chestnuts										•	•	•
clementine	•	•								•	•	•
cucumbers						•	•	•	•			
eggplants						•	•	•	•	•		
fennels	•	•	•	•	•					•	•	•
figs						•	•	•	•			
grapefruits	•	•	•	•	•						•	•
grapes								•	•	•	•	•
green bean					•	•	•	•	•			
kiwi	•	•	•	•	•						•	•
lemons	•	•	•	•						•	•	•
mandarins	•	•									•	•
melons					•	•	•	•	•			
oranges	•	•	•	•							•	•
peaches						•	•	•	•	•		
pears	•	•	•	•	•			•	•	•	•	•
peppers						•	•	•	•	•		
persimmon fruit									•	•	•	•
plums or prunes						•	•	•	•			
potatoes	•	•	•	•	•	•	•	•	•	•	•	•
pumpkins	•	•						•	•	•	•	•
raspberries					•	•	•	•	•	•		
scallion			•	•	•	•						
sour cherries						•	•	•				
strawberries				•	•	•						
tomatoes						•	•	•	•			
watermelons							•	•				
zucchini						•	•	•	•			

13

14

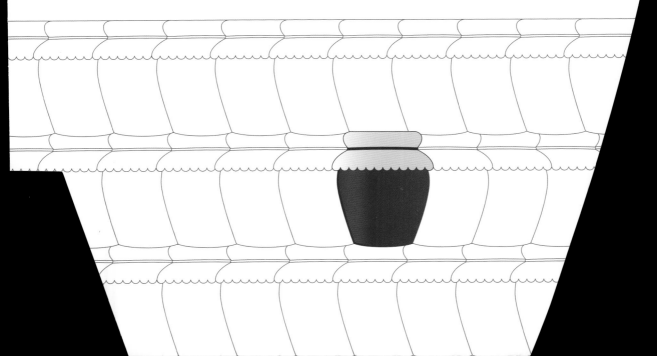

JAMS, MARMALADES AND JELLIES

VANILLA APRICOT JAM

INGREDIENTS FOR THREE 3/5 LB. (300 G) JARS

2 1/4 lbs. (1 kg) apricots
2 1/2 cups (500 g) sugar
1 vanilla pod, split lengthwise, seeds scraped

METHOD

Wash, pit and chop apricots. Combine apricots and sugar in a glass or metal bowl. Cover and allow to stand for 3 hours. Transfer to a large pan and simmer for 30 minutes, stirring constantly. Add vanilla pod to apricots and simmer for 15 minutes more, stirring constantly. Check jam consistency by pouring some on a plate, jam should not run too fast but it should be sticky and quite thick.

CANNING INSTRUCTIONS

To sterilize empty jars, partially fill a boiling-water canner with hot water. Place clean jars right side up on the rack into the boiling-water canner. Fill the canner and jars with hot (not boiling) water to 1 inch above the tops of the jars. Cover and bring water to a boil over high heat. Boil for at least 10 minutes (or up to 30 minutes, depending on canner size) at altitudes of less than 1,000 feet; at higher elevations, boil 1 additional minute for each additional 1,000 feet. Remove and drain hot sterilized jars one at a time. Save the hot water for processing lids and filled jars. Five minutes before you are ready to fill the jars, place lids in boiling water according to manufacturer's directions. Ladle preserve into the sterilized canning jars, leaving 1 inch of headroom. Be sure there are no air bubbles in the jar. Wipe the rims, put on the lids, and screw on the bands fingertip tight. Put jars in a large pot fitted with a canning rack. Add enough water to cover the jars by 2 to 3 inches. Bring the water to a boil over high heat, then lower the heat to maintain a rolling boil. Boil jars for 40 minutes. Be sure the jars are covered with water the entire time. Turn off the heat. Wait 5 minutes and then use a jar lifter to transfer jars to a rack or towel and let cool. If the seal is not tight, refrigerate and use within 10 days. If seal is tight, date jars and store them in a cool, dry place. The preserves will keep, unopened and at room temperature, for up to 1 year. After opening, store in refrigerator. Use within 10 days.

Preparation time: 15' - Resting time: 3 h - Cooking time: 45'
Difficulty: easy

SOUR CHERRY JAM

INGREDIENTS FOR THREE 3/5 LB. (300 G) JARS

2 1/4 lbs. (1 kg) cleaned and pitted sour cherries
3 1/3 lbs. (1.5 kg) sour cherries
to be cleaned and pitted
4 cups (800 g) sugar
2/3 cup (150 ml) water
Juice of 1 lemon

METHOD

Combine sugar and water in a large pan and bring to a boil.
Add cherries and lemon juice. Simmer for 45 minutes, stirring constantly.
Skim foam from top if needed. If you prefer smoother jam,
run through a food processor or a food mill.
Check jam consistency by pouring some on a plate,
jam should not run too fast but it should be sticky and quite thick.

CANNING INSTRUCTIONS

See canning instructions on page 16.

Preparation time: 15' - Cooking time: 45'
Difficulty: easy

FIG AND GINGER JAM

INGREDIENTS FOR TWO 9 OZ. (250 G) JARS

2 1/4 lbs. (1 kg) figs
1 3/4 cup (350 g) sugar
1 piece of root ginger, peeled and ground (optional)

METHOD

Peel figs and combine them with sugar and root ginger.
Simmer for 45 minutes, stirring constantly.
Check jam consistency by pouring some on a plate,
jam should not run too fast but it should be sticky and quite thick.

CANNING INSTRUCTIONS

See canning instructions on page 16.

Preparation time: 25' - Cooking time: 45'
Difficulty: easy

STRAWBERRY
AND LIME JAM

INGREDIENTS FOR THREE 3/5 LB. (300 G) JARS

2 1/4 lbs. (1 kg) strawberries
4 cups (800 g) sugar
Zest of 1 lime

METHOD

Wash strawberries. Drain well on a cloth.
Squeeze the lime. Once drained, cut strawberries into pieces.
Combine strawberries, sugar, lime zest and juice in a pan.
Simmer for 45 minutes, stirring constantly.
Check jam consistency by pouring some on a plate,
jam should not run too fast but it should be sticky and quite thick.

CANNING INSTRUCTIONS

See canning instructions on page 16.

Preparation time: 15' - Cooking time: 45'
Difficulty: easy

BERRY
JAM

INGREDIENTS FOR THREE 9 OZ. (250 G) JARS

9 oz. (250 g) currants
9 oz. (250 g) raspberries
9 oz. (250 g) blackberries
9 oz. (250 g) blueberries
4 cups (800 g) sugar

METHOD

Clean and wash berries, hull currants. Drain all berries on a cloth.
Combine berries and sugar in a glass or metal bowl.
Cover and allow to stand in a cool place for at least 3 hours (better overnight).
Transfer the mixture to a large pan and simmer for 45 minutes, stirring constantly.
Check jam consistency by pouring some on a plate,
jam should not run too fast but it should be sticky and quite thick.

CANNING INSTRUCTIONS

See canning instructions on page 16.

Preparation time: 15' - Resting time: 3-12 h - Cooking time: 45'
Difficulty: easy

PISTACHIO RASPBERRY JAM

INGREDIENTS FOR FIVE 1/2 LB. (200 G) JARS
2 1/4 lbs. (1 kg) raspberries
3 1/2 oz. (100 g) peeled pistachios nuts
4 cups (800 g) sugar
Zest of 1 lime

METHOD
Hull and wash raspberries. Drain on a cloth.
Combine raspberries and sugar in a glass or metal bowl and allow
them to stand in a cool place for 3 hours. Separate raspberries from sugar.
Put in a large pan sugar and the liquid left in the bowl. Reduce the liquid.
Add raspberries and lime zest. Cook for 45 minutes, stirring constantly.
Check jam consistency by pouring some on a plate,
jam should not run too fast but it should be sticky and quite thick.

CANNING INSTRUCTIONS
See canning instructions on page 16.

Preparation time: 15' - Resting time: 3 h - Cooking time: 45'
Difficulty: easy

MANGO, PEACH AND
CHILI PEPPER JAM

INGREDIENTS FOR FIVE 9 OZ. (250 G) JARS

3 lbs. (1.3 kg) mangoes
3/5 lb. (300 g) peaches
2 1/2 cups (500 g) sugar
1 chili pepper

METHOD

Peel mangoes and slice the flesh away from the core. Peel, pit and slice peaches.
Combine peaches, mangoes and sugar in a glass or metal bowl.
Cover and allow to stand in a cool place for 3 hours.
Transfer the mixture to a large pan and simmer for 45 minutes,
stirring constantly. Add chili pepper as much as you like.
Check jam consistency by pouring some on a plate,
jam should not run too fast but it should be sticky and quite thick.

CANNING INSTRUCTIONS

See canning instructions on page 16.

Preparation time: 15' - Resting time: 3 h - Cooking time: 45'
Difficulty: easy

APPLE
CINNAMON JAM

INGREDIENTS FOR THREE 1/2 LB. (200 G) JARS

2 1/4 lbs. (1 kg) apples
2 1/2 cups (500 g) sugar
Juice of 1 lemon
1 cinnamon stick

METHOD

Peel, core and chop apples. Combine apples, lemon juice,
sugar and cinnamon stick. Simmer for 45 minutes, stirring constantly.
Check jam consistency by pouring some on a plate,
jam should not run too fast but it should be sticky and quite thick.
Discard cinnamon (optional).

CANNING INSTRUCTIONS

See canning instructions on page 16.

Preparation time: 20' - Cooking time: 45'
Difficulty: easy

BLUEBERRY JAM

INGREDIENTS FOR THREE 3/5 LB. (300 G) JARS
2 1/4 lbs. (1 kg) blueberries
3 1/2 cups (700 g) sugar
1 lemon

METHOD
Hull and wash blueberries. Drain well on a cloth.
Combine blueberries and sugar in a glass or metal bowl
and allow to stand in a cool place for 12 hours.
Transfer the mixture to a suitable pan. Add juice and grated lemon zest
(only the yellow portion) and simmer for 45 minutes, stirring constantly.
Check jam consistency by pouring some on a plate,
jam should not run too fast but it should be sticky and quite thick.

CANNING INSTRUCTIONS
See canning instructions on page 16.

Preparation time: 10' - Resting time: 12 h - Cooking time: 45'
Difficulty: easy

ROSEMARY PEACH JAM

INGREDIENTS FOR TWO 3/5 LB. (300 G) JARS

2 1/4 lbs. (1 kg) yellow peaches
2 1/2 cups (500 g) sugar
1 sprig rosemary

METHOD

Peel, pit and chop peaches.
Combine peaches and sugar in a glass or metal bowl.
Cover and allow to stand in a cool place for at least 3 hours.
Transfer the mixture to a large pot and simmer,
stirring constantly, for 30 minutes.
Add as many rosemary leaves as you like and simmer for 15 minutes more.
Check jam consistency by pouring some on a plate,
jam should not run too fast but it should be sticky and quite thick.

CANNING INSTRUCTIONS

See canning instructions on page 16.

Preparation time: 20' - Resting time: 3 h - Cooking time: 45'
Difficulty: easy

GREEN TOMATO JAM

INGREDIENTS FOR 9 OZ. (250 G) JARS

1 lb. (500 g) green tomato
1 cup unpacked (150 g) brown sugar
1 lemon

METHOD

Wash, seed and cut tomatoes in 1/4 inch (0.5 cm) strips.
Combine tomatoes and sugar in a glass or metal bowl.
Cover with a film and allow to stand for 12 hours. Transfer the mixture to a pan.
Wash and drain lemon. Add juice and grated zest.
Simmer for 45 minutes, stirring often until the consistency is thick.

CANNING INSTRUCTIONS

See canning instructions on page 16.

Preparation time: 15' - Resting time: 12 h - Cooking time: 45'
Difficulty: easy

PUMPKIN JAM

INGREDIENTS FOR FOUR 12 OZ. (350 G) JARS

1 2/3 lb. (750 g) cooked pumpkin
(double that amount of raw pumpkin)
5 cups unpacked (700 g) brown sugar
5 tbsp. (70 ml) water
Juice of 1/2 lemon

METHOD

Wash pumpkin. Remove the rind and cut in small pieces.
Remove seeds and pith. Steam for half an hour
or until it is soft (you can also cook it in a cooker for 3-5 minutes).
Allow to cool, then run through a food mill or a processor.
Weigh 1 2/3 pound (750 g). Add sugar and allow to stand for an hour.
Add water and bring to a boil. Add juice of half lemon.
Boil for 5 minutes.

CANNING INSTRUCTIONS

See canning instructions on page 16.

Preparation time: 1 h - Resting time: 1 h - Cooking time: 5'
Difficulty: easy

QUINCE
JELLY

INGREDIENTS FOR 10 INCH (25 CM) DIAMETER BAKING PAN

2 1/4 lbs. (1 kg) quince
4 cups (800 g) sugar
Juice of 1 lemon
Water

METHOD

Peel, core and chop quinces.
Combine quinces and juice in a large pan. Fill the pot full with water.
Boil for about 20 minutes. Drain any left water and run through a food
mill or a blender. Return to the pan. Add sugar and simmer for about
20 minutes, stirring constantly. When the consistency is thick,
ladle into a baking pan sprinkled with sugar and
spread to be about 1 inch (2.5 cm) thick.
Let jelly sit until set to next day, then cut and shape as desired.

Preparation time: 30' - Cooking time: 40' - Resting time: 1 day
Difficulty: medium

BLACKBERRY JELLY

INGREDIENTS FOR THREE 5 1/2 TO 7 OZ. (150/200 G) JARS

2 1/4 lbs. (1 kg) blackberries
3 1/2 cups (700 g) sugar
1/2 cup (100 ml) water
Juice of 1 lemon

METHOD

Hull and wash blackberries, drain well on a cloth.
Once drained, combine them with sugar in a glass or metal bowl.
Cover and allow to stand in a cool place for 12 hours.
Transfer the mixture to a large pan.
Add water and simmer for half an hour, stirring constantly.
At half cooking sieve or strain through muslin, then add lemon juice.
Check jelly consistency by pouring some on a plate,
jam should not run too fast but it should be sticky and quite thick.

CANNING INSTRUCTIONS

See canning instructions on page 16.

Preparation time: 20' - Resting time 12 h - Cooking time: 30'
Difficulty: easy

BLACK CURRANT JELLY

INGREDIENTS FOR FIVE 3 1/2 OZ. (100 G) JARS

2 1/4 lbs. (1 kg) black currants
3 3/4 cups (750 g) sugar
1/2 cup (100 ml) water

METHOD

Hull and wash black currants. Put them in a large pan over the heat.
Add water and simmer for about 10 minutes, crushing berries with a spoon.
Strain through muslin and keep simmering for about 40 minutes,
stirring and skimming off foam from the top.
Check jelly consistency by pouring some on a plate,
jam should not run too fast but it should be sticky and quite thick.

CANNING INSTRUCTIONS

See canning instructions on page 16.

Preparation time: 10'- Cooking time: 45-50'
Difficulty: easy

ROSE
JELLY

INGREDIENTS FOR TWO 1/2 LB. (200 G) JARS

2 1/4 lbs. (1 kg) Russet apples
3 cups (750 ml) water
3 3/4 cups (750 g) sugar
8 roses
Juice of 1 lemon

METHOD

Wash roses and drain on a cloth.
Remove petals and combine them with sugar in a bowl.
Peel, core and chop apples. Put apples in a large pan with water and simmer,
stirring constantly, until they are reduced to pulp. Strain through muslin.
Add sugar, rose petals and lemon juice. Simmer for about half an hour, stirring.
Check jelly consistency by pouring some on a plate,
jam should not run too fast but it should be sticky and quite thick.

CANNING INSTRUCTIONS

See canning instructions on page 16.

Preparation time: 20' - Cooking time: 1 h 15'
Difficulty: easy

ORANGE MARMALADE

INGREDIENTS FOR TWO 9 OZ. (250 G) JARS

2 1/4 lbs. (1 kg) unwaxed oranges
3 cups (600 g) sugar
1 apple

METHOD

Wash oranges carefully.
Peel half of them and cut peel into thin strips.
Put peels in a small pan with some water. As soon as water boils, turn off the burner and change water. Repeat for three times. Peel oranges. With a very sharp knife separate segments scraping off the pith and keep segments in the fridge. Peel and dice the apple. Combine sugar, apple dices and orange juice from squeezed discarded parts in a high rim pan over medium heat.
When apple has reached setting point, add peeled oranges and peels.
Stir the marmalade often and sometimes skim off foam.
Check marmalade consistency by pouring some on a plate,
marmalade should not run too fast but it should be sticky and quite thick.

CANNING INSTRUCTIONS
See canning instructions on page 16.

Preparation time: 30' - Cooking time: 45'
Difficulty: medium

LEMON
MARMALADE

INGREDIENTS FOR TWO 16 OZ. (500 G) JARS

2 1/4 lbs. (1 kg) unwaxed lemons
4 cups (800 g) sugar

METHOD

Wash lemons carefully.
Place them in a pan full of water. Once reached a full rolling boil,
keep it for about 15 minutes. Drain and cool lemons. Wash and remove ends.
Quarter lemons lengthwise. Discard piths and chop segments roughly,
keeping the running juice. Combine lemons and sugar in a pan.
Simmer for about 20 minutes, stirring constantly.
Check marmalade consistency by pouring some on a plate,
marmalade should not run too fast but it should be sticky and quite thick.

CANNING INSTRUCTIONS

See canning instructions on page 16.

Preparation time: 20' - Cooking time: 45'
Difficulty: easy

PLUM
JAM

INGREDIENTIS FOR THREE 9 OZ. (250 G) JARS

2 1/4 lbs. (1 kg) plums
3 1/2 cups (700 g) sugar
1 lemon

METHOD

Clean and wash plums. Drain on a cloth, then pit and chop them.
Peel lemon and squeeze. Combine fruit and sugar in a glass or metal bowl.
Allow to stand in a cool place for at least 3 hours.
Transfer the mixture to a large pan. Add lemon juice and zest.
Simmer for about half an hour, stirring constantly.
Check jam consistency by pouring some on a plate,
jam should not run too fast but it should be sticky and quite thick.

CANNING INSTRUCTIONS

See canning instructions on page 16.

Preparation time: 20' - Resting time: 3 h - Cooking time: 30'
Difficulty: easy

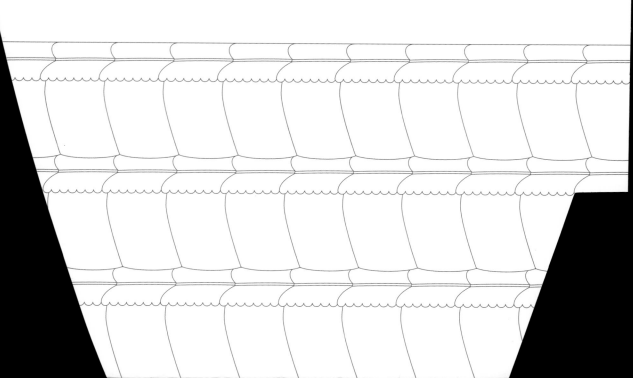

54

CANNED
FRUITS

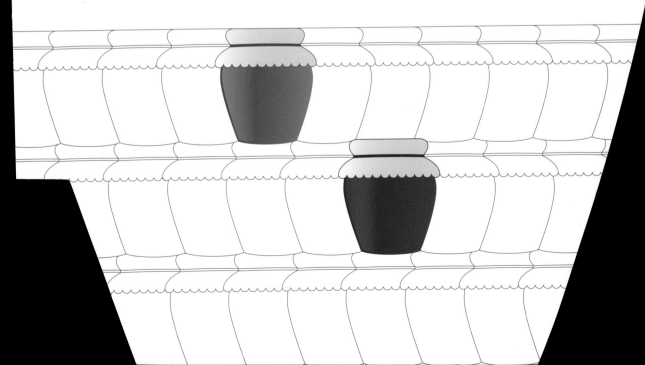

APRICOTS
IN SYRUP

INGREDIENTIS FOR TWO 16 OZ. (500 G) JARS

2 1/4 lbs. (1 kg) ripe but firm apricots
1 3/4 cup (350 g) sugar
4 cups (1 l) water

METHOD

Clean and wash apricots. Drain on a clean cloth.
Halve and pit them (you can leave 1-2 piths in each jar to flavor the syrup).
Place apricots in jars with airtight seal.
For syrup: dissolve sugar in water in a pan
and boil for about 2 minutes. Allow to cool.
Pour into jars and seal.

CANNING INSTRUCTIONS

See canning instructions on page 16.

Preparation time: 20'
Difficulty: easy

SOUR CHERRIES
IN SYRUP

INGREDIENTS FOR FOUR 3/5 LB. (300 G) JARS

2 1/4 lbs. (1 kg) sour cherries
2 cups (400 g) sugar
4 cups (1 l) water

METHOD

Clean and wash cherries. Drain on a clean cloth and remove stems.
For the syrup: dissolve sugar in water in a pan and boil for about 2 minutes.
Pack cherries into glass storage jars with airtight seal.
Cover with syrup and seal.

CANNING INSTRUCTIONS

See canning instructions on page 16.

Preparation time: 10'
Difficulty: easy

PINEAPPLE
IN SYRUP

INGREDIENTS FOR TWO 16 OZ. (500 G) JARS

1 pineapple
1 3/4 cup (350 g) sugar
4 cups (1 l) water
2 star anises

METHOD

Clean and peel pineapple. Remove the core of the pineapple.
Cut into 1/2 inch (1 cm) thick slices, then pack them into
jars with large mouth. For the syrup: dissolve sugar in water
in a pan and boil together with star anises for about 2 minutes.
Let it cool. Pour into the jars and seal.

CANNING INSTRUCTIONS

See canning instructions on page 16.

Preparation time: 20'
Difficulty: easy

CHESTNUTS IN SYRUP

INGREDIENTS FOR TWO 3/5 LB. (300 G) JARS

2 1/4 lbs. (1 kg) chestnuts
3 1/2 cups (700 g) sugar
1/2 cup (200 g) corn syrup
1 vanilla pod, split lengthwise, seeds scraped
4 cups (1 l) water

METHOD

Make a cut along chestnuts and put in a colander over a pan with
boiling water so that steam makes peeling easy, then remove the shell.
Place chestnuts in some pieces of cheesecloth tied with thread
and simmer until you can prick them with a toothpick.
Once cooked or still boiling hot, remove skin. Meanwhile, prepare
syrup with water, sugar, and corn syrup. Add vanilla pod to mixture.
Boil for 5 minutes. Place chestnuts on a small rack that can be set in
a container such as a high rim baking tin or a bowl. Cover with boiling syrup
and keep in a warm place. Next day remove the rack with chestnuts.
Boil syrup for 3 minutes, then pour on chestnuts again. Repeat this procedure
for 7 or 8 days, adding additional syrup if needed. Pack chestnuts into clean
and dry jars. Boil syrup and pour into jars to fill them up. Seal.

CANNING INSTRUCTIONS

See canning instructions on page 16.

Preparation time: 8-9 days
Difficulty: medium

BRANDIED CHERRIES

INGREDIENTS FOR FOUR 3/5 LB. (300 G) JARS

2 1/4 lbs. (1 kg) cherries
1 1/4 cup (250 g) sugar
2 cups (500 ml) Brandy
1/4 cup (50 ml) water
1 clove

METHOD

Wash cherries and drain on a clean cloth.
Cut and destem the cherries.
Pack cherries into clean and dry jars with airtight seal.
For the syrup: dissolve sugar with water in a pan and boil
for about 2 minutes with clove. Let cool then add brandy.
Pour the syrup into the jars and seal. Let cherries stand in alcohol
in a cool, dark place for at least 1 month before eating.

Preparation time: 20' - Resting time: 30 days
Difficulty: easy

HAZELNUTS
IN ACACIA HONEY

INGREDIENTS FOR THREE 3/5 LB. (300 G) JARS

1 lb. (500 g) shelled hazelnuts
1 3/4 cup (600 g) acacia honey

METHOD

Toast hazelnuts in the oven at 350°F (180°C) for about 10 minutes until
the dark skin can be peeled off easily. Place hazelnuts on a clean cloth.
Let cool for a few minutes, then scrub to remove skin.
Fill the jars three quarters full with the prepared hazelnuts.
Place them in the oven at 210°F (100°C).
Meanwhile, in a pan heat honey at about 210°F (100°C),
then pour into jars to fill them up.
Adjust lids and turn jars upside down immediately to form headspace
to improve preservation. Place jars upside down until cooled completely.
Store in a cool, dry place.

Preparation time: 40'
Difficulty: easy

PEARS IN
RED WINE

INGREDIENTS FOR TWO 1 2/3 LB. (750 G) JARS

2 1/4 lbs. (1 kg) small but firm pears
4 cups (1 l) red wine
2 1/2 cups unpacked (350 g) brown sugar
2-3 cloves
1 piece of cinnamon stick

METHOD
Peel pears and pack into jars.
Meanwhile, in a small pan boil wine, sugar, few cloves and a piece
of cinnamon stick, then pour the syrup over pears. Put on lids.

CANNING INSTRUCTIONS
See canning instructions on page 16.

Preparation time: 20' - Resting time: 20'
Difficulty: easy

PEACHES
IN SYRUP

INGREDIENTS FOR TWO 16 OZ. (500 G) JARS
2 1/4 lbs. (1 kg) firm peaches
2 cups (400 g) sugar
2 1/2 cups (600 ml) water
1 vanilla pod, split lengthwise, seeds scraped
Zest of 1 lemon
2 cloves

METHOD
Wash peaches. Place in a pan with boiling water for half a minute.
Drain and let cool with water and ice in a bowl to peel them easily
(if nectarines are used, avoid boiling because they must not be peeled).
Cut the peaches in half, pit and drain on a clean cloth.
For the syrup: dissolve sugar in water and add the vanilla pod,
zest cut into strips and cloves. Boil 2 minutes for flavor, then remove.
Pack peaches into jars with airtight seal. Cover with syrup and seal.

CANNING INSTRUCTIONS
See canning instructions on page 16.

Preparation time: 2 h
Difficulty: easy

CANNED
SUGARFREE PLUMS

INGREDIENTS FOR FIVE 1/2 LB. (200 G) JARS

2 1/4 lbs. (1 kg) plums
Zest of 1 lemon
2 cloves
1 piece of cinnamon stick

METHOD

Wash and drain plums with clean cloth. Cut the fruit in half,
pit them and pack them carefully into jars with airtight seal.
Add lemon zest cinnamon and cloves, then seal.

CANNING INSTRUCTIONS

See canning instructions on page 16.

Preparation time: 20'
Difficulty: easy

CANDIED ORANGE PEELS

INGREDIENS FOR THREE 12 OZ. (350 G) JARS

4 1/2 lbs. (2 kg) oranges with thick peel
3 3/4 cups (750 g) sugar
2/5 cup (150 g) corn syrup
1 vanilla pod, split lengthwise, seeds scraped
4 cups (1 l) water

METHOD

Wash and drain oranges. Score the peel of each orange
into quarters, and pull the quarters of peel off the orange.
Keep peels in running water for at least 24 hours.
Boil the peels over medium heat and when it is possible
prick with the point of a knife (it takes about half an hour).
Drain and place in a pile in a container.
For syrup: combine water, sugar, and corn syrup.
Add vanilla pod to mixture together with its scraped seeds.
Boil for 5 minutes, then pour immediately over peels.
Put on a small grid or a holed lid to keep peels immersed
in the syrup and keep in a warm place.
Next day drain syrup from the container and boil for about 3 minutes.
Pour over peels again. Repeat this procedure for about 12 days,
adding additional syrup if needed. Finally pack peels into clean and dry jars.
Boil syrup and pour into jars to fill them up. Seal.

CANNING INSTRUCTIONS
See canning instructions on page 16.

See canning instructions on page 16.

Preparation time: 13 days
Difficulty: medium

76

CANNED
VEGETABLES

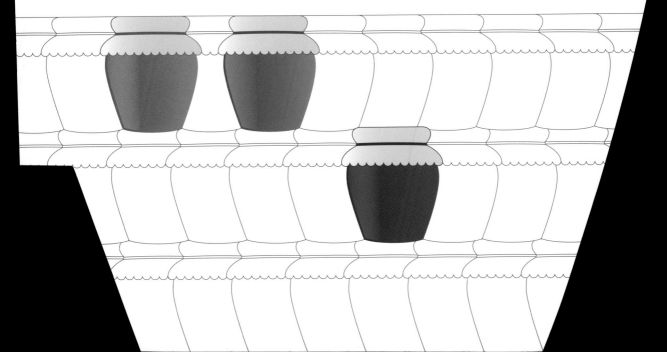

CANNED ASPARAGUS

INGREDIENTS FOR 1 2/3 LB. (750 G) JAR

2 1/4 lbs. (1 kg) asparagus
3 tsp./4 cups (15 g/l) salt
1 tbsp./4 cups (1 tbsp./l) vinegar
2 cups (500 ml) water

METHOD

Wash asparagus. Trim and scrape off woody bases.
Tie them up in small bunches and blanch in salted boiling
water for 5 minutes. Drain and cool in ice water.
Pack into jar, tips up not to damage them.
Combine boiled water, vinegar (a tablespoon per 4 cups)
and salt (about 3 teaspoons per 4 cups)
and fill the jar with this liquid. Put on the lid.
Check to make sure the jar was properly sealed.
Use a pressure canner to process it
(check the manufacturer's directions and canning instructions).
Follow maintenance and storage instructions
that come from your canner manufacturer.

Preparation time: 30'
Difficulty: easy

ARTICHOKES
IN OIL

INGREDIENTS FOR TWO 3/5 LB. (300 G) JARS

2 1/4 lbs. (1 kg) artichokes
2 cups (500 ml) vinegar
1 cup (250 ml) water
1 cup (250 ml) white wine
1 lemon
2 garlic cloves
2 bay leaves
Peppercorns
Few juniper berries
Dried oregano
1 tsp. coriander
1 clove
2 tsp. (10 g) salt
Extra virgin olive oil

METHOD

Clean artichokes by slicing at least 1/4 inch (0.5 cm) off the tops and bottoms
and removing all the tough outer leaves. Cut the artichokes in half lengthwise.
Remove the chokes. Cut into thin slices and soak in a bowl of water
with the lemon juice to prevent the artichokes from turning black.
Meanwhile, in a pan boil vinegar with all ingredients except for artichokes and oil.
When liquid comes to full rolling boil, blanch artichokes for 5 minutes,
then drain through a colander and put them on a cloth to dry.
Pack artichokes into sterilized jars,
putting same flavors used in cooking in each jar.
Fill up with oil. Let liquid sit and add additional oil if needed.
Put on lids carefully. Keep refrigerated or process the jars
according to canning instructions.

Preparation: 1 h 30'
Difficulty: easy

PICKLES

INGREDIENTS FOR TWO 16 OZ. (500 G) JARS

2 1/4 lbs. (1 kg) gherkins
4 tbsp. (50 g) sugar
4 cups (1 l) white vinegar at least 5% acidity (50 grain)
2 sprigs tarragon
1 tbsp. mustard seeds
Peppercorns
Salt

METHOD

Clean and wash gherkins. Place in a container and completely cover with salt.
Let stand for 12 hours. After that, boil vinegar with sugar, tarragon sprigs
and some peppercorns. Blanch cucumbers in vinegar for few seconds.
Drain through a skimmer and pack into clean and dry jars.
Add mustard seeds. Return vinegar mixture to boiling,
then strain the hot vinegar (to remove spices) into jars.
Let cool and adjust lids.

CANNING INSTRUCTIONS

See canning instructions on page 16.

Preparation time: 30' - Resting time: 12 h
Difficulty: easy

PICKLED ONIONS

INGREDIENTS FOR TWO 16 OZ. (500 G) JARS

2 1/4 lbs. (1 kg) scallions
2 1/2 tbsp. (30 g) sugar
1/4 cup plus 2 tbsp. (80 ml) balsamic vinegar at least 5% acidity (50 grain)
2 bay leaves
2 cloves (optional)
Peppercorns
Salt

METHOD

Peel, clean and wash scallions. Combine balsamic vinegar,
sugar, salt, bay leaves and few cloves (optional) in a pan.
Bring to a boil. Blanch scallions for few seconds. Drain through a skimmer.
Pack into clean and dry jars. Return vinegar mixture to boiling,
then strain the hot vinegar (to remove spices) into jars.
Let cool and adjust lids.

CANNING INSTRUCTIONS

See canning instructions on page 16.

Preparation: 30'
Difficulty: easy

GREEN BEANS

INGREDIENTS FOR FOUR 16 OZ. (500 G) JARS

2 1/4 lbs. (1 kg) green beans
3 tsp./4 cups (15 g/l) salt
1 tbsp./4 cups (1 tbsp./l) vinegar
2 cups (500 ml) water

METHOD

Remove ends and strings from green beans. Wash and drain.
Pack into jars and cover with brine made with boiled water, vinegar
(a tablespoon per 4 cups) and salt (about 3 teaspoons per 4 cups).
Put on lids. Check to make sure the jars were properly sealed.
Use a pressure canner to process them
(check the manufacturer's directions and canning instructions).
Follow maintenance and storage instructions
that come from your canner manufacturer.

Preparation time: 20'
Difficulty: easy

PICKLED VEGETABLES

INGREDIENTS FOR THREE 3/5 LB. (300 G) JARS

1 lb. (500 g) cauliflower
3/5 lb. (300 g) carrots
5 1/2 oz. (150 g) peppers
7 oz. (200 g) scallions
7 oz. (200 g) cucumbers
2 cups (500 ml) vinegar at least 5% acidity (50 grain)
2 1/2 tbsp. (30 g) sugar
Wild fennel (optional)
Peppercorns
Salt

METHOD

Clean and wash all vegetables. Cut cauliflower into florets.
Cut cucumbers into evenly sliced rounds. Cut peppers into
diamond-shaped pieces and julienne carrots or cut into a shape you like.
In a pan combine vinegar, sugar, salt, few peppercorns
and wild fennel (optional) and boil.
Blanch each type of vegetables separately with vinegar but keep
them crunchy, then pack them in alternate layers into glass jars.
Return liquid to a boil and pour it still boiling over vegetables.
Let cool and adjust lids.

CANNING INSTRUCTIONS
See canning instructions on page 16.

Preparation time: 30' - Cooking time: 15'
Difficulty: easy

EGGPLANT
IN OIL

INGREDIENTS FOR TWO 16 OZ. (500 G) JARS

2 1/4 lbs. (1 kg) eggplants
2 cups (500 ml) vinegar
2 garlic cloves sliced
Extra virgin olive oil
Basil leaves
Oregano (fresh or dried)
Salt

METHOD

Wash eggplants and slice into about 1/5 inch (5 mm) thick slices.
Salt and sit in a colander for about an hour to pull out juice with bitter flavor.
In a pan bring vinegar to a boil and blanch eggplant slices
for a couple of minutes, then drain and place on a cloth to dry.
Pack eggplant into clean and dry jars.
Add few basil leaves, sliced garlic cloves and a pinch of oregano.
Fill up with extra virgin olive oil, let the liquid set and add additional oil if needed.
Put on lids carefully. Keep refrigerated or process the jars
according to canning instructions.

Preparation time: 1 h 30'
Difficulty: easy

SWEET AND SOUR PEPPERS

INGREDIENTS FOR THREE 3/5 LB. (300 G) JARS

2 1/4 lbs. (1 kg) peppers
1 1/4 cup (250 g) sugar
2 cups (500 ml) vinegar at least 5% acidity (50 grain)
2 cups (500 ml) white wine
2 bay leaves
Peppercorns
Salt

METHOD

Wash and clean peppers. Remove seeds and membrane, then slice.
Combine white wine, vinegar, a pinch of salt, bay leaves and peppercorns in a pan.
Bring to a boil and blanch peppers for 2-3 minutes. Drain through a skimmer
and pack into clean and dry jars. Strain vinegar mixture.
Return liquid to a boil, add sugar, boil for about 2 minutes,
then strain into jars. Put on lids.

CANNING INSTRUCTIONS

See canning instructions on page 16.

Preparation time: 40'
Difficulty: easy

CANNED
PEELED TOMATOES

INGREDIENTS FOR TWO 16 OZ. (500 G) JARS

2 1/4 lbs. (1 kg) San Marzano tomatoes
1 sprig of fresh basil
Salt
Sugar

METHOD

Wash tomatoes. Make a cut along them with a paring knife, then blanch
for 30 seconds in a pan with boiling water. Drain through a colander,
then cool tomatoes in a bowl with ice water to remove skin easily.
Pack into jars with airtight seal. Salt them slightly
and add a pinch of sugar. Flavor with basil and seal.

CANNING INSTRUCTIONS

See canning instructions on page 16.

Preparation time: 30'
Difficulty: easy

BOLETE MUSHROOMS
IN OIL

INGREDIENTS FOR THREE 1/2 LB. (200 G) JARS

2 1/4 lbs. (1 kg) small and firm boletes
2 cups (500 ml) vinegar
2 garlic cloves
2 bay leaves
Some juniper berries
2 cloves
Black peppercorns
4 tsp. (20 g) salt
Extra virgin olive oil

METHOD

Clean mushrooms by rubbing the debris from the bottom with a paring knife
and wipe them with a damp cloth. In a pan combine vinegar
and all ingredients except for boletes and oil and bring to a boil.
When the liquid comes to a full rolling boil, blanch mushrooms
for a few minutes, drain them through a strainer and place on a cloth to dry.
Pack mushrooms into clean, dry jars.
Fill up with oil, let the level of liquid set and add additional oil if needed.
Put on lids carefully. Keep refrigerated or process the jars
according to canning instructions.

Preparation time: 1 h 30'
Difficulty: easy

BOTTLED
TOMATO SAUCE

INGREDIENTS FOR 1 2/3 LB. (750 G) SAUCE

2 1/4 lbs. (1 kg) San Marzano tomatoes

METHOD

Wash tomatoes, make a cut along them with a paring knife,
then blanch for 30 seconds in a pan with boiling water.
Drain through a strainer and cool in a bowl with ice water to remove skin easily.
Press tomatoes through a food mill (or through the appropriate tool)
to discard skin and seeds. Fill bottles and seal.

CANNING INSTRUCTIONS

See canning instructions on page 16.

Preparation time: 1 h
Difficulty: easy

SAUCES AND MOSTARDA

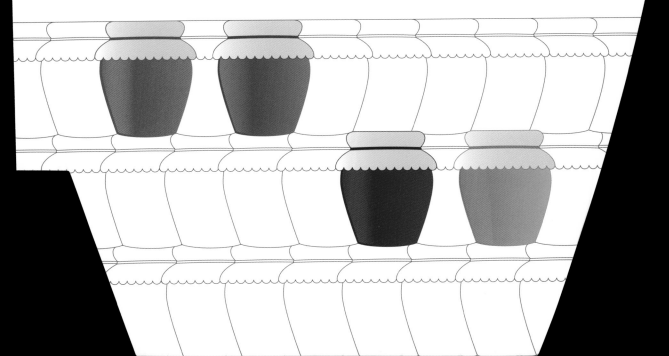

COGNÀ
(PICKLED CANDIED FRUITS
IN A SYRUP)

INGREDIENTS FOR EIGHT 16 OZ. (500 G) JARS
2 1/2 gallons (10 l) grape juice
3 1/3 lbs. (1.5 kg) quinces
3 1/3 lbs. (1.5 kg) pears (russet pears)
3 1/3 lbs. (1.5 kg) peaches or plums
15 fresh figs (or 10 dried figs)
3/5 lb. (300 g) walnut kernels
3/5 lb. (300 g) toasted hazelnuts
3/5 lb. (300 g) almonds
Zest of 3 lemons
10-12 cloves
5-6 centimeter long cinnamon stick

METHOD
Boil grape juice and reduce it by about half.
Add chopped fruits as follows: quinces, pears, peaches,
figs and dried fruit, then put spices into a spice bag.
Cook for at least 4 hours, stirring constantly, then pack into glass canning jars.

CANNING INSTRUCTIONS
See canning instructions on page 16.

Preparation time: 20' - Cooking time: 4-5 h
Difficulty: easy

CHERRY CHUTNEY

INGREDIENTS FOR FIVE 3 1/2 OZ. (100 G) JARS

2 1/4 lbs. (1 kg) cleaned and pitted cherries
(about 3 1/3 lbs. - 1.5 kg - cherries to be cleaned and pitted)
3 cups unpacked (450 g) brown sugar
2 tbsp. (30 ml) balsamic vinegar

METHOD

Place cherries in a glass or metal bowl, add sugar,
cover and let stand in a cool place for about 3 hours.
After that transfer the mixture to a large pan and simmer
for about half an hour, stirring constantly
and skimming foam from the top if needed.
Check chutney consistency by pouring some on a plate,
jam should not run too fast but it should be sticky and quite thick.
Add balsamic vinegar.

CANNING INSTRUCTION

See canning instructions on page 16.

104

Preparation time: 15' - Cooking time: 30'
Difficulty: easy

RED ONION CHUTNEY

INGREDIENTS FOR 9 OZ. (250 G) JAR

4/5 lb. (400 g) red onions
2/3 cup (150 ml) red wine
1/3 cup unpacked (50 g) brown sugar
1/2 tbsp. (10 g) acacia honey

METHOD

Peel and chop onions finely.
In a pan combine onions, honey, wine and sugar and simmer
over low heat for about 45 minutes, then pack into the jar.
Keep refrigerated or process the jar according to canning instructions.

CANNING INSTRUCTIONS

See canning instructions on page 16.

Preparation time: 15' - Cooking time: 45'
Difficulty: easy

GINGERED PEAR PRESERVE

INGREDIENTS FOR FOUR 1/2 LB. (200 G) JARS

2 1/4 lbs. (1 kg) pears
1 1/2 cup (300 g) sugar
2 limes
3/4 cup plus 2 tbsp. (200 ml) water
1 piece of root ginger

METHOD

Peel pears. Core, chop or dice them.
Combine pears, sugar, water, ground ginger and lime juice in a large pan.
Simmer for about half an hour, stirring constantly.
Check preserve consistency by pouring some on a plate,
preserve should not run too fast but it should be sticky and quite thick.

CANNING INSTRUCTION

See canning instructions on page 16.

Preparation time: 20' - Cooking time: 45'
Difficulty: easy

HOMEMADE KETCHUP

INGREDIENTS FOR TWO 5 1/2 OZ. (150 G) JARS

2 1/4 lbs. (1 kg) San Marzano tomatoes
5 1/2 oz. (150 g) onions
3 1/2 oz. (100 g) carrots
3 1/2 oz. (100 g) celery
5 tsp. (25 ml) extra virgin olive oil
1/3 cup plus 2 tbsp. (100 ml) water
1/2 cup (120 ml) red vinegar at least
5% acidity (50 grain)

3 1/2 oz. (100 g) brown sugar
3/4 oz. (20 g) tomato paste
1 garlic clove
2 chili peppers (fresh or dried)
1 bay leaf
3 basil leaves
1 sprig thyme
Salt and pepper

METHOD

Wash tomatoes. Make a cut along them with a paring knife.
Blanch for 30 seconds in a pan with boiling water. Drain through
a skimmer. Cool them in a bowl with ice water to remove skin easily.
Halve them. Discard seeds and chop. Clean all vegetables and cut them finely.
Heat oil in a large pan and cook chopped vegetables. Add chili peppers,
garlic clove and basil, then add tomatoes, herbs, tomato paste and water.
Season. Bring to a boil and simmer for about 30 minutes.
Add sugar and vinegar and finish cooking, it takes about
1 hour in all. Discard bay leaf and run through food processor. If needed,
further reduce mixture to the consistency of ketchup. Fill jars and seal.

CANNING INSTRUCTION

See canning instructions on page 16.

Preparation time: 1 h - Cooking time: 1 h
Difficulty: easy

MOSTARDA
FROM CREMONA

INGREDIENTS FOR TWO 3/5 LB. (300 G) JARS

2 1/4 lbs. (1 kg) mixed fruit (pears, cherries, figs, apricots)
2 1/2 cups (500 g) sugar
mustard seeds or powder

METHOD

Peel and chop fruit. Place in a bowl and sprinkle with sugar.
Let stand for about 24 hours.
Drain liquid from the bowl into a small pan and boil for about
10 minutes, then return juice to the bowl with fruits.
Let stand for 24 hours and repeat procedure for 5 days in all.
On fifth day boil juice and fruits for 5 minutes.
Add mustard seeds or powder (adjust dose according to your taste)
and pack into glass canning jars. Put on lids.

CANNING INSTRUCTION
See canning instructions on page 16.

Preparation time: 5 days
Difficulty: medium

WATERMELON
CHUTNEY

INGREDIENTS FOR FOUR 5 1/2 OZ. (150 G) JARS

3 1/3 lbs. (1.5 kg) watermelon
2 1/2 cups (500 g) sugar
mustard seeds or powder

METHOD

Cut and scrape flesh from zest and discard seeds.
Chop into 2 centimeter wide pieces.
Place in a glass or metal bowl and sprinkle with sugar.
Let stand for 24 hours. Drain the liquid from the jars into a small pan
and boil for about 10 minutes, then pour boiling syrup over watermelon.
Let stand for about 24 hours and repeat procedure for 4 times in all.
Finally boil syrup and watermelon together for 5 minutes.
Add mustard seeds or powder (adjust dose according to your taste)
and pack into glass canning jars. Put on lids.

CANNING INSTRUCTION

See canning instructions on page 16.

Preparation time: 4 days
Difficulty: easy

FIG CHUTNEY

INGREDIENTS FOR TWO 9 OZ. (250 G) JARS

2 1/4 lbs. (1 kg) figs
1 3/4 cup (350 g) sugar
mustard seeds or powder

METHOD

Peel and quarter figs. Combine figs and sugar in a glass or metal bowl.
Let stand for about 24 hours. Drain the juice from the bowl into a small pan
and boil for about 10 minutes, then pour boiling syrup over figs.
Let stand for further 24 hours and repeat procedure.
Let stand for further 24 hours, this time boil figs and juice until figs form a pulp.
Add mustard seeds or powder (adjust dose according to your taste)
and pack into glass canning jars. Put on lids.

CANNING INSTRUCTION
See canning instructions on page 16.

Preparation time: 3 days
Difficulty: easy

MELON
CHUTNEY

INGREDIENTS FOR SIX 5 1/2 OZ. (150 G) JARS

4 1/2 lbs. (2 kg) melon
2 1/2 cups (500 g) sugar
Zest of 1 lemon
mustard seeds or powder

METHOD

Cut melon. Scrape flesh and discard seeds.
Chop pulp into about 4/5 inch (2 cm) wide pieces.
Place them in a glass or metal bowl and sprinkle with sugar.
Let stand for about 24 hours. Drain juice from the bowl.
Combine it with lemon zest (without the white portion as it is sour)
and boil for about 10 minutes, then pour boiling syrup over melon.
Let stand for 24 hours and repeat procedure for 3 times in all.
Finally boil syrup and fruit for 15 minutes.
Discard zest and run through a food mill or processor.
Add mustard seeds or powder (adjust dose according to your taste)
and pack into glass canning jars. Put on lids.

CANNING INSTRUCTION
See canning instructions on page 16.

Preparation time: 4 days
Difficulty: easy

MOSTARDA
FROM MANTOVA

INGREDIENTS FOR TWO 3/5 LB. (300 G) JARS

2 1/4 lbs. (1 kg) quinces (or Russet apples)
2 1/2 cups (500 g) sugar
mustard seeds or powder

METHOD

Peel and slice apples. Place in a bowl and sprinkle with sugar.
Let stand for 24 hours. Drain juice from the bowl into a small pan
and boil for about 10 minutes, then return it to apples.
Let stand for further 24 hours and repeat procedure.
Let stand for further 24 hours, then boil apples and juice for 5 minutes.
Add mustard seeds or powder (adjust dose according to your taste)
and pack into glass canning jars. Put on lids.

CANNING INSTRUCTION

See canning instructions on page 16.

Preparation time: 32 days
Difficulty: easy

ALPHABETICAL INDEX
OF RECIPES

ALPHABETICAL INDEX
OF INGREDIENTS

All the photographs are by Academia Barilla except
©123RF: timer image; Africa Studio/Shutterstock: page 128; belchonock/iStockphoto: page 9;
Floortje/iStockphoto: page 10; Isantilli/Shutterstock: pages 122, 123;
photomaru/iStockphoto: cover; Andris Tkacenko/Shutterstock: page 7;
Voronin76/Shutterstock: pages 5, 13, 125, 126; YingYang/iStockphoto: page 2

ACADEMIA BARILLA
ITALIAN GASTRONOMIC AMBASSADOR
TO THE WORLD

In the heart of Parma, recognized as one of the most prestigious capitals of cuisine, the Barilla Center stands in the middle of Barilla's historical headquarters, now hosting Academia Barilla's modern structure. Founded in 2004 with the aim of affirming the role of Italian culinary arts, protecting the regional gastronomic heritage, defending it from imitations and counterfeits and to valorize the great tradition of Italian cooking, Academia Barilla is where great professionalism and unique competences in the world of cuisine meet. The institution organizes cooking courses for those passionate about food culture, offering services dedicated to the operators in the sector and proposing products of unparalleled quality. Academia Barilla was awarded the "Business-Culture Prize" for its promotional activities regarding gastronomic culture and Italian creativity in the world. Our headquarters were designed to meet the educational needs in the field of food preparation and has the multimedia tools necessary to host large events: around an extraordinary gastronomic auditorium, there is an internal restaurant, a multisensory laboratory and various classrooms equipped with the most modern technology. In our Gastronomic Library we conserve over 11,000 volumes regarding specific topics and an unusual collection of historical menus and printed materials on the culinary arts: the library's enormous cultural heritage is available online and allows anyone to access hundreds of digitalized historical texts. This forward thinking organization and the presence of an internationally renowned team of professors guarantee a wide rage of courses, able to satisfy the needs of both catering professionals as well as simple cuisine enthusiasts. Academia Barilla also organizes cultural events and initiatives for highlighting culinary sciences open to the public, with the participation of experts, chefs and food critics. It also promotes the "Cinema Award", especially for short-length films dedicated to Italian food traditions.

www.academiabarilla.it

WHITE STAR PUBLISHERS

WS White Star Publishers® is a registered trademark
property of De Agostini Libri S.p.A.

© 2014 De Agostini Libri S.p.A.
Via G. da Verrazano, 15
28100 Novara, Italy
www.whitestar.it - www.deagostini.it

Translation and editing: Maria Cristina Ferrari e C. s.a.s.

ISBN 978-88-544-0824-1
1 2 3 4 5 6   18 17 16 15 14

Printed in China

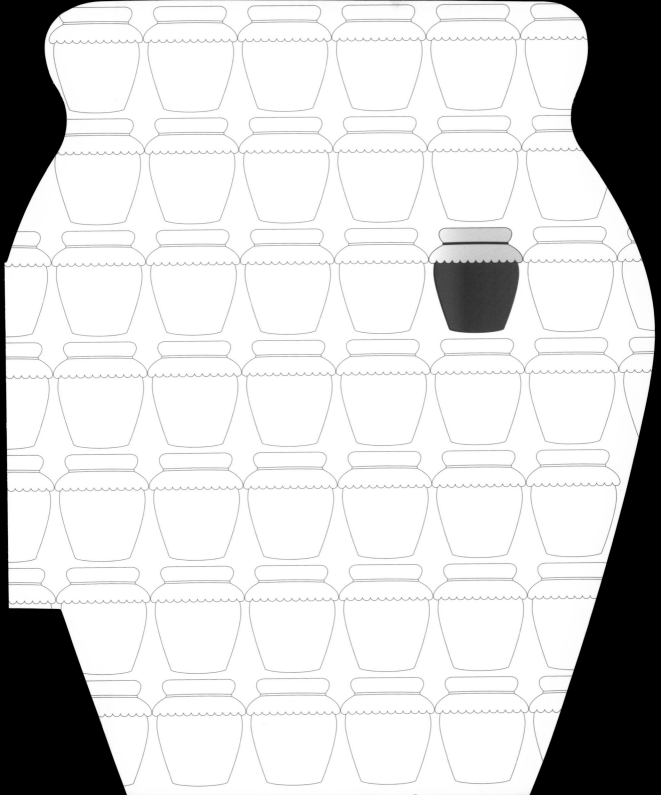

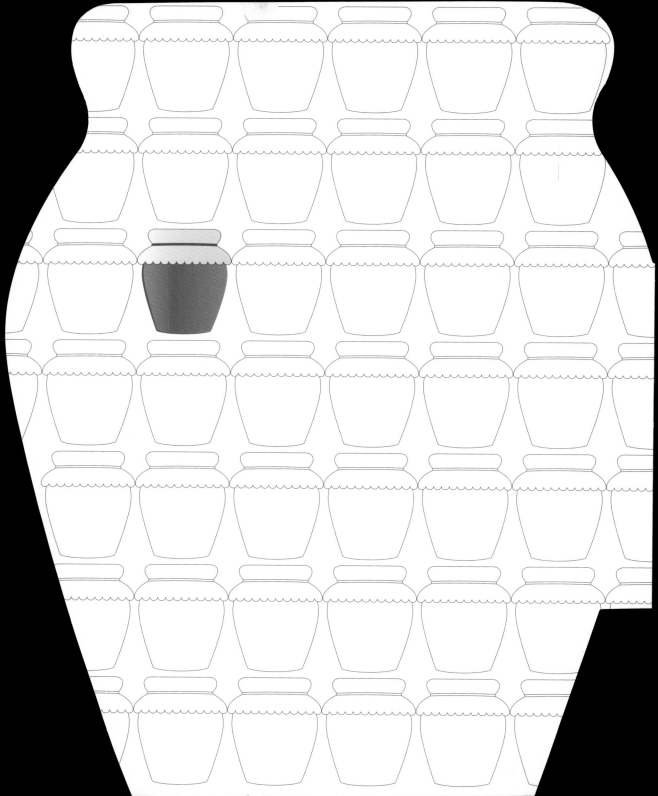